Executive Branch
of the Government

Written by Julia Hargrove

Illustrated by Bron Smith

Teaching & Learning Company

1204 Buchanan St., P.O. Box 10
Carthage, IL 62321-0010

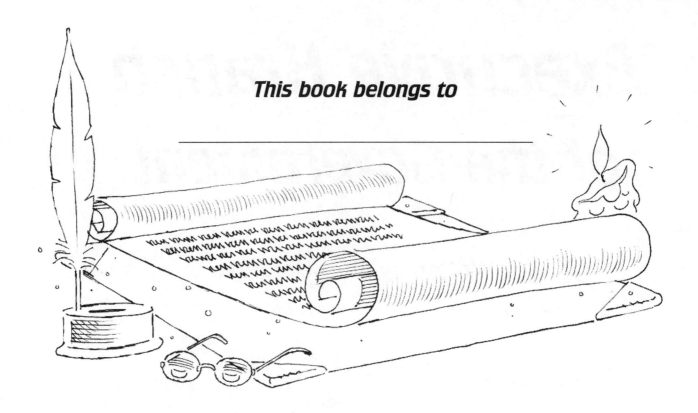

This book belongs to

_____

Cover photo courtesy Library of Congress archives

Copyright © 2000, Teaching & Learning Company

ISBN No. 1-57310-243-1

Printing No. 987654

Teaching & Learning Company
1204 Buchanan St., P.O. Box 10
Carthage, IL 62321-0010

Table of Contents

Article II–Executive Department. 5

Presidential Amendments 8

Executive Department Questions 9

Presidential and Constitutional Trivia 10

Presidential Powers and Duties 11

Presidential Roles. 13

Separation of Powers 15

Checks and Balances 17

Checks and Balances Questions. 18

Presidential Cabinet. 19

Presidential Cabinet Questions 21

Presidential Ranking. 22

Steps in Presidential Impeachment Trial 24

Mock Impeachment Trials–Historical Suggestions 25

Internet Research Ideas 28

Multiple Intelligence Activities. 30

Answer Key. 32

Dear Teacher or Parent,

This book is one in a series by the Teaching & Learning Company on the three branches of the United States government. Together the three will show the powers of each branch, how they interact with one another in a system requiring separation of powers and how each branch is designed to prevent the other two branches from assuming too much power.

It is important that young people understand their national government because that government is working for them and for all citizens. However, it cannot do the best job possible without the participation of its citizens. Certainly we look to the government to solve many of our problems: to provide emergency relief after natural disasters, to defend us from foreign enemies, to make sure the food we eat is wholesome and the medicine we take is effective, to take care of us in our old age and to help provide money for schools for our young people. In return, we have our responsibilities, too. We must pay our taxes; vote in elections; be well informed about candidates and national issues when we vote; let our representatives, senators and the President know our opinions about pending legislation and act as watchdogs when the government is not working for our best interests. One of the ways we can help young people to grow into responsible citizens is to help them understand how their government works.

This book about the Executive Branch explains the powers and duties of the President and the roles the President plays as leader of our country. It also contains Article II of the Constitution, which created the Executive Department, information about the Cabinet, a role-playing game about impeachment and many other activities. I hope you find the book useful and a worthy challenge of your students' abilities.

Sincerely,

Julia

Julia Hargrove

Article II–Executive Department

Section I. President and Vice President

1) The executive power shall be vested in a President of the United States of America. He shall hold his office during the term of four years, and, together with the Vice President, chosen for the same term, be elected as follows:

2) Each State shall appoint, in such manner as the legislature thereof may direct, a number of electors, equal to the whole number of Senators and Representatives to which the State may be entitled in the Congress; but no Senator or Representative, or person holding an office of trust or profit under the United States, shall be appointed an elector.

3) The Congress may determine the time of choosing the electors and the day on which they shall have their votes; which day shall be the same throughout the United States.

4) No person except a natural-born citizen shall be eligible to the office of President; neither shall any person be eligible to that office who shall not have attained to the age of thirty-five years, and been fourteen years a resident within the United States.

5) In case of the removal of the President from office or of his death, resignation, or inability to discharge the powers and duties of the said office, the same shall devolve on the Vice President, and the Congress may by law provide for the case of removal, death, resignation, or inability, both of the President and Vice President, declaring what officer shall then act as President, and such officer shall act accordingly, until the disability be removed, or a President shall be elected.

Section I. President and Vice President

1) The head of the Executive Branch will be the President of the U.S. The President's term of office will be four years. The Vice President's term is also four years. Both officers will be elected as follows:

2) Each state will appoint its electors according to the method decided by the state legislature. Each state will have the same number of electors as the number of its representatives and senators combined. No elector can be a senator, representative or any other officer in a paid job or a position of trust in the U.S. government.

3) The U.S. Congress can determine the date when the electors vote. That date must be the same in every state in the United States.

4) Any person elected to be President must be a natural-born citizen of the U.S., at least 35 years old and have lived in the U.S. for 14 years.

5) In case of removal from office, death, resignation or inability of the President to carry out his duties, the Vice President will become President. Congress will decide the order of succession if neither the President nor the Vice President can serve. The successor will be President until the President is able to serve again or a new President is elected.

Article II–Executive Department

6) The President shall, at stated times, receive for his services a compensation, which shall neither be increased nor diminished during the period for which he shall have been elected, and he shall not receive within that period any other emolument from the United States, or any of them.

7) Before he enter on the execution of his office, he shall take the following oath or affirmation: "I do solemnly swear (or affirm) that I will faithfully execute the office of the President of the United States, and will to the best of my ability preserve, protect and defend the Constitution of the United States."

Section II. Powers of the President

1) The President shall be commander in chief of the army and navy of the United States, and of the militia of the several States, when called into the actual service of the United States; he may require the opinion, in writing, of the principal officer in each of the executive departments, upon any subject relating to the duties of their respective offices, and he shall have power to grant reprieves and pardons for offenses against the United States, except in cases of impeachment.

2) He shall have power, by and with the advice and consent of the Senate, to make treaties, provided two-thirds of the Senators present concur, and he shall nominate, and by and with the advice and consent of the Senate, shall appoint ambassadors, other public ministers and consuls, judges of the Supreme Court, and all other officers of the United States, whose appointments are not herein otherwise provided for, and which shall be established by law: but the Congress may by law vest the appointment of such inferior officers, as they think proper, in the President alone, in the courts of law, or in the heads of departments.

6) The President will be paid at certain times. His pay will not be raised or lowered during his time in office. He also cannot receive any other money from the United States or any individual states.

7) The President will take this oath of office before he takes over the job. "I swear that I will faithfully carry out my job as President of the U.S. I will also protect and defend the U.S. Constitution."

Section II. Powers of the President

1) The President is the highest commander of the army and navy. He is also the commander of the states' militias when they serve the whole nation. He can require information from the heads of his Cabinet departments. He can grant reprieves and pardons in all cases except impeachment.

2) The President can make treaties. The Senate must approve the treaty by a two-thirds vote. He can appoint ambassadors, ministers, consuls and Supreme Court judges, but the Senate must approve those appointments. He can appoint all other officers not mentioned in the Constitution but created by law. Congress can decide which officers can be appointed by the President, the courts or the heads of departments without Senate approval.

Article II–Executive Department

3) The President shall have power to fill up all vacancies that may happen during the recess of the Senate, by granting commissions that shall expire at the end of their next session.

Section III. Other Powers and Duties of the President

1) He shall from time to time give to the Congress information of the state of the Union, and recommend to their consideration such measures as he shall judge necessary and expedient; he may, on extraordinary occasions, convene both houses, or either of them, and in case of disagreement between them, with respect to the time of adjournment, he may adjourn them to such time as he shall think proper; he shall receive ambassadors and other public ministers; he shall take care that the laws be faithfully executed, and shall commission all the officers of the United States.

Section IV. Impeachment

1) The President, Vice President and all civil officers of the United States shall be removed from office on impeachment for, and on conviction of, treason, bribery, or other high crimes and misdemeanors.

3) Some appointments to positions in the Executive Branch require the consent of the Senate. If one of these offices becomes vacant during a time when the Senate is not meeting, the President may appoint someone to fill that office without the approval of the Senate. The appointment is good until the end of the next session of the Senate.

Section III. Other Powers and Duties of the President

1) The President must periodically give Congress information about the state of the United States. He can recommend laws that he would like to have passed. In an emergency, he can call Congress back into session. If the two houses of Congress disagree about when to adjourn, the President can adjourn them for a given time. He shall receive ambassadors from foreign countries. He must make sure the laws are carried out and enforced. He approves the promotion to a higher rank for all military officers.

Section IV. Impeachment

1) The President, Vice President and all other U.S. officers can be impeached for treason, bribery or other high crimes or misdemeanors. If they are convicted of the charges, they will be removed from office.

Presidential Amendments (Paraphrased)

Amendment XII: Election of the President and Vice President (1804)

Amendment XII changed the way the President and Vice President are elected by the Electoral College. The candidates for President are now to be voted on separately from the candidates for Vice President. After the votes are counted, the results are sent to the President of the Senate, who opens the certificates from the Electoral College and counts the votes in front of the members of the Senate and the House of Representatives. The person with the highest number of votes for President becomes President, and the person with the highest number of votes for Vice President becomes Vice President.

Amendment XX: Presidential and Congressional Terms (1933)

Amendment XX changed the date of the President's inauguration from March 4 to January 20. It reduced the time between the election and the date the new President takes office, thus reducing the time a "lame duck" (powerless) President remains in office.

Amendment XXII: Anti-Third Term Amendment (1951)

No person can be elected President more than twice. No person who has acted as President for more than two years of a previous President's term can be elected President more than once. This does not apply to the President in office when this amendment is ratified.

Amendment XXV: Presidential Succession and Disability (1967)

1) If the President dies, resigns or is removed from office, the Vice President becomes President.

2) If there is no Vice President, the President shall nominate someone to fill that job. The nominee then must be confirmed by a majority of both Houses of Congress before becoming Vice President.

3) If the President sends a written message to the Senate's President Pro Tempore and the Speaker of the House saying that he is unable to carry out his duties, the Vice President shall become Acting President.

4) The President can also be declared incapable of carrying out his duties if the Vice President and the majority of the Cabinet members agree that he is disabled. They then send the required written statement to the Senate's President Pro Tempore and the Speaker of the House. The Vice President becomes Acting President.

5) If the President writes a declaration to the Senate's President Pro Tempore and the Speaker of the House saying that he is no longer disabled, he will become the President unless the Vice President and a majority of the Cabinet disagree with the President. If the Vice President and the Cabinet say the President is still disabled, Congress decides the issue. If two-thirds of both houses of Congress agree that the President is disabled, the Vice President continues as Acting President. If the Congress does not reach a two-thirds majority, the President returns to his job.

Executive Department Questions

Answer the following questions in the spaces provided. Your answers must be sentences.

1. If a person wants to be President or Vice President, what three qualifications must he or she meet?

   _____

   _____

2. How is the number of electors figured for each state? How many electors does your state have?

   _____

   _____

3. How long is one term in office for a President? How many terms can a President have in office? If a Vice President takes over for a President with only a year left in his or her term, how many times can that Vice President be President in his or her own right? (See Amendment 22.)

   _____

   _____

4. Any change Congress makes in the President's salary cannot apply to the person who is President when the law is passed. Why do you think the Constitution has this rule?

   _____

   _____

5. What are two powers of the President that require the advice and consent of the Senate?

   _____

6. What are three duties of the President?

   _____

   _____

7. Does the Constitution describe the duties and powers of the Vice President? If so, tell what those duties and powers are.

   _____

8. a. What process can be used to remove the President from office for committing crimes?

   _____

   b. What process can be used to remove the President from office if he or she is too disabled to carry out the duties of the President? (See Amendment 25.)

   _____

   _____

Name _____

Presidential and Constitutional Trivia

These questions cover real-life situations related to the Constitution's Executive Department and various amendments about the President. Answer each question below. An explanation of why your answer is correct is required to make your answer complete.

1. The House Judiciary Committee had drawn up impeachment charges against President Nixon, but he resigned before the House impeached him. President Ford later pardoned Nixon. How could Ford pardon a person in an impeachment case?

   _____

2. President Truman served all except a few months of President Roosevelt's fourth term and then was elected to another term in his own right. The 22nd Amendment was ratified during Truman's second term. Could Truman have run for President a second time?

   _____

3. During the Civil War, President Lincoln issued the Emancipation Proclamation freeing slaves in certain areas of the South. He used his power as commander in chief to make the Proclamation. Why was this the best power for him to use under the circumstances?

   _____

4. Former Vice President Aaron Burr was tried for treason for a scheme to take over some land belonging to the U.S. and forming his own country. At his trial, one of Burr's coconspirators testified against him. Why was Burr not convicted of the treason charges?

   _____

5. Madeline Albright, President Clinton's Secretary of State, was born in Czechoslovakia and came to the United States as a child. She is a U.S. citizen, over 35 and experienced in government offices. All of the Cabinet members are in the line of succession to the presidency. Could Mrs. Albright have become President, even if the opportunity arose?

   _____

6. In 1824 when John Quincy Adams, Andrew Jackson, Henry Clay and William H. Crawford ran for President, there was no candidate with a clear majority of electoral votes after the election. What process was used to choose Adams as President?

   _____

7. The Constitution continually refers to the President and Vice President as "he." Is there anything in Article II that prevents a woman from being elected to these offices?

   _____

8. President Woodrow Wilson suffered a severe stroke while on a speaking tour to promote the League of Nations in 1919. He was so ill that his wife virtually ran the Executive Branch during the remainder of Wilson's second term. If the 25th Amendment had been in the Constitution in 1919, would Wilson have completed his second term as President?

   _____

Name _____

Presidential Powers and Duties

I. Powers of the President

1. He is commander in chief of the U.S. army and navy (but cannot declare war).
2. He is commander in chief of the militias of the states when those troops are called into national service.
3. He may require the opinions of the heads of his Cabinet departments on any subject related to their work.
4. He can grant reprieves and pardons in all cases except impeachments.
5. He can make treaties with foreign countries (with the approval of the Senate).
6. He can appoint ambassadors, ministers, consuls and other envoys to foreign countries (with the approval of the Senate).
7. He can appoint Supreme Court justices (with the approval of the Senate).
8. He can appoint all other officers of the U.S. (with the approval of the Senate).
9. He can appoint senators to fill vacancies that occur during the recess of the Senate.
10. He can recommend to Congress laws that he wants to have passed.
11. He can call both houses of Congress into session under special circumstances.
12. He can adjourn Congress if the two houses don't agree on a time to adjourn.

II. Duties of the President

1. He shall deliver to Congress information about the state of the Union.
2. He shall receive ambassadors and public ministers from foreign countries.
3. He shall make sure that the laws of the nation are faithfully carried out.
4. He shall commission all military officers of the United States.

III. Questions

If the President has the power or the duty to do the following actions, write *yes* in the blank provided. If the President cannot do the thing described, write *no* in the blank. Below the question, write the specific power that applies to that situation. If the President does not have that power, write *none*.

_____ 1. An enemy is invading the United States by attacking California. The U.S. does not have enough troops on the coast to fight this enemy, so the President requests the governor of California to call up its National Guard. The President then takes over the command of the Guard to help fight off the attack.

Power: _____

_____ 2. The President wants to recommend some new legislation to Congress during his State of the Union message. He requests the Secretary of Labor to research statistics on unemployment and the Secretary of Health and Human Services to find information about Social Security payments. He delivers this information during his speech.

Duty:_____   Power: _____

11

Presidential Powers and Duties

_____ 3. The President becomes frustrated with Supreme Court decisions that declare his programs to be unconstitutional. He decides to fire two of the justices and to increase the number of justices on the court to eleven.

Power: _____

_____ 4. The President asks the Internal Revenue System to harass some citizens he doesn't like by auditing their income tax returns every year that the President is in office.

Power: _____

_____ 5. The ambassador to Mexico negotiates a treaty to buy the Gadsden Purchase from Mexico in order to have an easy route on which to build a railroad. The President is pleased with the treaty and sends it to the Senate for ratification.

Power: _____

_____ 6. The Director of the FBI reports to the President that people are smuggling goods into the U.S. to avoid the customs taxes. The President orders the Director to arrest these criminals.

Duty: _____

_____ 7. President X appointed his friend Judge Y to the Supreme Court, and Congress confirmed the appointment. Later, Judge Y was impeached and convicted of taking a bribe in a Supreme Court case. President X pardoned his friend so that Judge Y could remain a justice on the court.

Power: _____

_____ 8. In 1979, President Carter sent military troops and helicopters to the Middle East on an operation to rescue the hostages being held prisoner in Iran.

Power: _____

_____ 9. The Secretary of State resigns from office in the middle of the President's term. The Senate is in recess for the Christmas and New Year's holidays. Because of the unsettled situation in the Middle East, the President needs a new Secretary of State immediately. He appoints a new head of the State Department without the consent of the Senate.

Power: _____

Presidential Roles

The Constitution gives the President many powers and duties. These can be grouped into seven roles: legislative leader, commander in chief of the military, foreign policy leader, judicial leader, chief of state, chief executive and political party leader.

A. **Legislative Leader:** Although Congress makes the laws, the President can suggest laws and persuade members of Congress to vote for them. Each year, the President gives the State of the Union Address in which he suggests ideas he would like to see made into laws. His staff prepares the budget, which Congress changes and approves. The President can send special messages to Congress suggesting laws, and he can call special sessions of Congress when emergencies arise.

B. **Commander in Chief of the Military:** The President is the highest authority in the U.S. military. The Joint Chiefs of Staff, the generals and admirals and all of the soldiers must do what the President tells them to do.

C. **Foreign Policy Leader:** The President, with the help of advisors, makes foreign policy. The President decides what relationship the U.S. will have with other countries: whether the U.S. will send them money, food, technology and military aid or treat them as our enemies. The President appoints ambassadors and other diplomats to foreign countries and can negotiate treaties or other agreements with them.

D. **Judicial Leader:** The President can appoint federal judges including Supreme Court justices and the Chief Justice. He can also grant pardons (end punishment for a crime), commute a sentence (change it to a lesser punishment) and grant reprieves (temporarily put off the date a punishment takes place).

E. **Chief of State:** In this role, the President is the symbol of the United States. He attends the funerals of foreign leaders, awards medals to worthy citizens, lights the nation's Christmas tree, greets foreign leaders when they visit the U.S. and performs other purely ceremonial duties.

F. **Chief Executive:** The President is the leader of the Executive Branch of the national government. For instance, he appoints or dismisses members of his Cabinet, oversees agencies and commissions under executive control, selects the members of his White House staff and works on the budget with his advisors.

G. **Political Party Leader:** The President is the most important member of his own political party. During an election year, he makes speeches and helps to raise money for party members running for offices such as governor, senator or representative.

COMMANDER
← in CHIEF

Name _____

Presidential Roles

Below are examples of presidential actions. Decide which role the President was fulfilling by each action, and put the letter of that role in the space provided. Some answers will be used more than once.

_____ 1. When young men and women graduate from West Point or the Air Force Academy, the President commissions them as officers in the United States military.

_____ 2. After World War I, President Wilson went to Europe to work with the leaders of Britain, France and Italy to write the peace treaties to end the war.

_____ 3. During the Hundred Days of Franklin D. Roosevelt's first administration in 1933, the President and his advisors suggested dozens of laws to Congress to improve conditions during the Great Depression.

_____ 4. President Truman fired General Douglas MacArthur during the Korean War. MacArthur wanted to invade China, which was supplying troops and weapons to North Korea; but Truman didn't want to risk a third world war by attacking China.

_____ 5. President Reagan appointed the first woman, Sandra Day O'Connor, to be a Supreme Court justice.

_____ 6. President Clinton appointed the first woman Attorney General, Janet Reno, and the first woman Secretary of State, Madeline Albright, to his Cabinet.

_____ 7. President Clinton honored Rosa Parks, a civil rights activist, at a ceremony shown on national television.

_____ 8. In 1978, President Carter brought Egypt's Sadat and Israel's Begin to the United States where they reached a peace agreement known as the Camp David Accords.

_____ 9. President Thomas Jefferson sent ships to the Mediterranean Sea to fight the Barbary pirates along the coast of North Africa without a declaration of war by Congress.

_____ 10. President Clinton attended the funeral of King Hussein of Jordan in 1999.

_____ 11. Although the U.S. ambassadors to France were only bargaining to purchase the city of New Orleans, Thomas Jefferson gave them permission to buy all of the Louisiana Territory when Napoleon offered to sell it for $15 million.

_____ 12. President Clinton toured the nation speaking for members of the Democratic party in the congressional elections of 1994.

_____ 13. President Franklin D. Roosevelt called a special session of Congress to ask that body to declare war against Japan after the bombing of Pearl Harbor.

14

Name _____

Separation of Powers

One of the most important concepts of the way the federal government works is called separation of powers. That means that each of the three branches has different powers and responsibilities in running the government. The purpose of separation of powers is to prevent any one leader or branch of government from taking over the whole power of government. The power is divided among the branches in this way: the legislative branch (Congress) makes the laws, the executive branch (President) carries out the laws and the judicial branch (Supreme Court) interprets the laws.

To say that Congress makes the laws means that senators and representatives pass legislation that makes certain ideas the law of the land. What is meant by the President's power to carry out the laws is that the executive is the law enforcement branch. The President has the power to use the military, the FBI and other agencies to make people obey the laws and to arrest people who don't obey them. The Supreme Court decides what the law means. The Court does this through trials in which the meaning of the law is argued by the prosecution and the defense. The Supreme Court justices then make a ruling on which side wins the case and what the law means.

Questions

For each of the situations described below and on the following page, decide whether it shows separation of powers or not. If it is an example of separation or powers, write *yes* in the space provided. If it is not an example, write *no* in the space.

_____ 1. Congress cannot pass bills of attainder. That means that they cannot pass a law that declares a person guilty of treason without having had a treason trial.

_____ 2. Congress can investigate its own members and punish them by censure or by expelling them from Congress.

_____ 3. The Supreme Court can only try cases that come under the original jurisdiction written in the Constitution or cases that are appealed to the Court. It cannot have people arrested and tried in the Supreme Court simply because it wants to make a test case about a specific law.

_____ 4. The President can issue Executive Orders that have the force of law and have to be obeyed by the people.

Separation of Powers

_____ 5. The Federal Bureau of Investigation and the Alcohol, Tobacco and Firearms agency can arrest people they think have violated federal laws. However, after the arrests, the FBI or ATF must turn the people over to the court system to be tried for the crimes they are accused of committing.

_____ 6. The President in the annual State of the Union Address can suggest to Congress laws that he would like to see passed, but he cannot make these ideas into laws on his own.

_____ 7. The Supreme Court ruled in 1954 in Brown vs. Board of Education of Topeka, Kansas, that African American students had to be allowed to attend formerly all-white schools. When Arkansas refused to follow this decision, President Eisenhower sent troops to Little Rock to escort the African American students into Central High School and to protect them from the violence of white mobs.

_____ 8. Congress passes tax laws raising or lowering the amount of money citizens pay to the government, but the collection of taxes and enforcement of laws is the responsibility of the Internal Revenue Service in the Executive Branch of the government.

_____ 9. There are certain types of cases that the Supreme Court must hear according to the Constitution; however, in all other cases, the justices decide themselves which cases they are going to try.

Checks and Balances

The idea of checks and balances works with separation of powers to prevent a single leader or any one of the branches from taking total control of the federal government. Checks and balances are written into the Constitution. They give each branch some powers over the other two branches so that each branch can help check or prevent the other two from gaining all the power in the government. For instance, the President can appoint Supreme Court justices, but the Senate has the power to confirm or reject the President's appointments. That way, the President can't control the Supreme Court by appointing his friends and making the Court automatically support anything he wants to do. Below are examples of checks that each branch has over the other two.

A. Executive Branch (President)

1. He appoints Supreme Court justices.
2. He can veto laws passed by Congress.
3. He is commander in chief of the military and can move troops to danger spots throughout the world.
4. He has the power to grant pardons and reprieves and to commute the sentences of criminals.

B. Legislative Branch (Congress)

1. The Senate confirms the appointments of Supreme Court justices.
2. Congress can overturn a presidential veto by two-thirds vote of both houses.
3. The Senate ratifies treaties made by the President or his ambassadors.
4. The Senate confirms appointments of ambassadors and other foreign representatives recommended by the President.
5. The House of Representatives impeaches the President; the Senate tries the President on impeachment charges.
6. Only Congress can declare war.
7. Only Congress can appropriate money to carry out laws or to pay for the President's movement of military troops overseas.

C. Judicial Branch (Supreme Court)

1. The Supreme Court can declare congressional laws and Executive Orders unconstitutional.
2. The Chief Justice of the Supreme Court presides over an impeachment trial of a President.

Checks and Balances Questions

The following questions are based on the information about checks and balances. If the situation described is an example of checks and balances (even if the two branches both agreed to the action), write *yes* in the blank provided. If it is not an example of checks and balances, write *no*.

_____ 1. When Mexico attacked U.S. troops in the area between the Nueces and Rio Grande Rivers in 1846, President Polk sent a message to Congress asking for a declaration of war against Mexico. Congress did declare war.

_____ 2. When President Clinton sent U.S. troops to Kosovo to stop the "ethnic cleansing" of minorities, Congress voted the money to pay for transportation, weapons, food and support services for the soldiers.

_____ 3. Ronald Reagan nominated Sandra Day O'Connor to the Supreme Court. Congress confirmed her appointment, and she became the first female Supreme Court justice.

_____ 4. In 1973-74, Congress investigated the events surrounding the Watergate break-in with the intention of finding out whether President Nixon was involved in the planning of the event or a cover-up after the event. Congress subpoenaed the tape recordings Nixon had made of conversations in the Oval Office of the White House. Nixon claimed he didn't have to give up the tapes because of executive privilege. The Supreme Court ruled that he did have to give the tapes to Congress.

_____ 5. Both the Senate and the House of Representatives have standing committees that investigate bills, question experts on specific topics and study the possible effects if the bill is passed. These committees then either "kill" a bill or present it to the full House for a vote.

18

Presidential Cabinet

The Constitution mentions a Cabinet indirectly when it says that the President can ask for the opinion, in writing, "of the principal officer in each of the executive departments." During George Washington's administrations, these executive departments developed into a group of advisors called the Cabinet. At first there were three department heads: the Secretaries of State, War and the Treasury. As the national government grew, the number of Cabinet departments increased to 14. Below is a list of departments in the order that they were created with a brief description of their responsibilities.

Department of State (1789)

The Secretary of State helps the President to decide on foreign policy and to negotiate treaties. He or she oversees the Foreign Service's ambassadors, ministers and consuls and helps tourists in foreign countries.

Department of War (1789)

The Secretary of Defense helps the President in his or her role as commander in chief of the military. He or she coordinates all branches of the military and advises the President in time of war. This Cabinet post was combined with the Department of the Navy to become the Department of Defense in 1947.

Department of the Treasury (1789)

The Secretary of the Treasury supervises all means the U.S. has of raising money including the Internal Revenue Service and the Customs Service. It also sells bonds to borrow money. The U.S. Mint prints and coins money. The Secretary is also involved in the development of the nation's budget. The Secret Service, which protects the lives of the President and his or her family, is part of this department.

Department of the Interior (1849)

Part of the duty of the Secretary of the Interior is to supervise the use of natural resources such as oil and mineral deposits that belong to the nation. Agencies in this department include the U.S. Fish and Wildlife Service, the National Parks Service and the U.S. Geological Survey. The Bureau of Indian Affairs handles issues concerning Native Americans.

Department of Agriculture (1862)

The overall purpose of this department is to help farmers. Examples of this are the Rural Electrification Administration and the Soil Conservation Service. The Secretary of Agriculture also oversees the school lunch program through the Food and Nutrition Service and the purity of the nation's food supply through the Animal and Plant Inspection Service.

Department of Justice (1870)

The Attorney General advises the President on legal matters. He or she aids the President in his or her role as chief executive, who carries out the laws and arrests those who break the laws. The Federal Bureau of Investigation, the Federal Marshals, the national prison system and the Immigration and Naturalization Services are examples of agencies that are part of the Department of Justice.

Department of Commerce (1903)

The Department of Commerce and Labor was split into two departments in 1913. The secretary of this department helps American businesses through such agencies as the Economic Development Administration and the International Trade Administration. The Patent and Trademark Office and National Weather Service are also part of the Commerce Department.

Presidential Cabinet

Department of Labor (1903)

The Secretary of Labor helps American workers, often with safety regulations such as those administered by the Occupational Safety and Health Administration and the Mine Safety and Health Administration. The Bureau of Labor-Management Relations supervises relations between workers and their bosses. Other agencies in this department include the Bureau of Labor Statistics and the Employment and Training Administration.

Department of Housing and Urban Development (1965)

Federal loans for mortgages, housing for the poor and equal rights in acquiring adequate housing are among the issues that concern this department. Assistant secretaries include those for Fair Housing and Equal Opportunity, Community Planning and Development and Public and Indian Housing. This department also helps cities to improve traffic control and plan for mass transportation services.

Department of Transportation (1966)

Some of the agencies in this department such as the Federal Aviation Administration, the National Highway Traffic Safety Administration and the Federal Railroad Administration regulate different methods of transportation. Another purpose of the department is to develop solutions to transportation problems. The Urban Mass Transportation Administration is an example of this function. During peacetime, the U.S. Coast Guard is also part of Transportation.

Department of Energy (1977)

The use and conservation of energy resources and the development of new types of energy are the responsibilities of this department. Different agencies handle fossil energy (coal and oil), nuclear energy (nuclear power plants) and renewable energy sources (sun, wind and water). Civilian Radioactive Waste Management sets standards for things like the disposal of radioactive materials used in nuclear medicine.

Department of Health and Human Services (1979)

This department began as Health, Education and Welfare in 1953 but was split in 1979. Its agencies fight the spread of infectious diseases such as AIDS, try to find cures for illnesses such as cancer and arthritis, oversee the testing and approval of new drugs and work to help persons with mental health problems. Among the agencies that do this work are the Centers for Disease Control, the Food and Drug Administration and the National Institute of Health.

Department of Education (1979)

While decisions about education are made on the local level by school boards and the voters who live in a school district, the federal government does provide money to public schools, conducts research on educational issues and makes recommendations to local school districts. Bilingual, vocational and adult education are among the concerns of this department.

Department of Veteran Affairs (1989)

This department replaced the Veterans Administration and gained Cabinet status under President Bush. The National Cemetery System, Veterans Benefits Administration and Veterans Health Services and Research Administration are among the agencies under this branch.

Presidential Cabinet Questions

For each of the topics below, write the name of the Cabinet department that would most likely deal with the issue.

1. During the oil embargo of the late 1970s, President Carter encouraged the development of other sources of power such as wind, the sun and shale oil.

   Cabinet Department: _____

2. The number of homeless people is increasing because of a lack of low-cost housing.

   Cabinet Department: _____

3. Many soldiers who fought in Vietnam developed diseases after being exposed to Agent Orange; soldiers who fought in the Gulf War showed symptoms called the Gulf War Syndrome. All of these men require medical treatment.

   Cabinet Department: _____

4. When previously unknown diseases appear, such as Legionaire's disease in the 1970s, AIDS in the 1980s and the hanta virus in the 1990s, federal agencies try to find the causes, methods of prevention and cures for these illnesses.

   Cabinet Department: _____

5. In 1977, President Carter resumed Strategic Arms Limitation Talks with the Soviet Union to reduce nuclear weapons in both the U.S. and the U.S.S.R.

   Cabinet Department: _____

6. Amtrak is a passenger railroad system owned and operated by the federal government.

   Cabinet Department: _____

7. The President is concerned about the rate of unemployment in the U.S. He wants statistics about the problem and suggestions on how to reduce it.

   Cabinet Department: _____

8. During Washington's first administration, Congress passed an excise tax on whiskey to raise money. Farmers in Pennsylvania protested the tax in what became known as the Whiskey Rebellion. Washington went to Pennsylvania to put down the rebellion and took with him the Cabinet secretary who had suggested the tax to Congress.

   Cabinet Department: _____

Presidential Ranking

Among historians' polls of the most able U.S. Presidents, George Washington, Thomas Jefferson, Andrew Jackson, Abraham Lincoln, Theodore Roosevelt, Woodrow Wilson and Franklin D. Roosevelt are usually given the highest rankings. You have a chance to express your opinions in this exercise. Work in small groups and follow the directions in each segment to reach your decision about who was the most able President. The culmination of this activity will be a class debate and final vote on the ranking of the best Presidents.

I. For each of the Presidents listed below, write several reasons why that person should be considered the best President ever. There is a space for a write-in vote so you can add your nominee for number one.

A. George Washington: _____

_____

B. Thomas Jefferson: _____

_____

C. Andrew Jackson: _____

_____

D. Abraham Lincoln: _____

_____

E. Theodore Roosevelt: _____

_____

F. Woodrow Wilson: _____

_____

G. Franklin D. Roosevelt: _____

_____

H. Write-In President (optional): _____

_____

Presidential Ranking

II. Vote in your small groups to determine who might be considered the top five Presidents of all time. Write your results below.

A. First Place: _____

B. Second Place: _____

C. Third Place: _____

D. Fourth Place: _____

E. Fifth Place: _____

III. In preparation for the class debate on who was the best President, write a paragraph with four or five arguments stating why your top choice should be elected number one. Each member of your small group must contribute at least one idea for this paragraph.

_____

_____

_____

_____

_____

_____

_____

_____

IV. Your teacher will conduct the debate on the best President and take a vote to determine the class's choice for number one.

Steps in Presidential Impeachment and Trial

Use these steps to conduct a mock impeachment and trial. Student roles in this process would include the members of the House Judiciary Committee, the House Managers, the Chief Justice of the Supreme Court, the President, the defense lawyers, witnesses and the Senate as a jury.

1. The Judiciary Committee of the House of Representatives studies the charges against the President and writes the articles of impeachment.

2. The whole House of Representatives examines and debates the articles of impeachment. The House then votes on whether to impeach the President and which articles of impeachment will be used to charge him or her.

3. The Senate holds the impeachment trial based on the charges delivered from the House of Representatives. All one hundred senators serve as the jury in the impeachment trial. They are not allowed to speak during the trial.

4. The senators take the following oath before the trial: "I solemnly swear (or affirm) that in all things appertaining to the trial of . . . , now pending, I will do impartial justice according to the Constitution and laws, so help me God."

5. Selected members of the House of Representatives, called managers, present the impeachment case to the Senate. Their role is like that of lawyers in a regular trial.

6. The President has his or her own lawyers to present his or her defense during the trial.

7. The Chief Justice of the Supreme Court is the presiding judge. He makes decisions about legal points and what evidence can be presented during the trial. He also relays questions from the senators to the House managers.

8. Both the prosecution and the defense may present witnesses to give evidence and to be cross-examined.

9. Two people on each side of the case (four people total) present the closing arguments.

10. After the prosecution and defense have finished their cases, the Senate goes into session to debate the President's guilt or innocence. Each senator is allowed 15 minutes to speak.

11. When the debate is over, the senators vote for or against the charges. A roll call vote is held, and each senator votes on each separate article of impeachment. A two-thirds vote is required to convict the President.

12. The penalty for conviction in an impeachment trial is removal from office.

Mock Impeachment Trials– Historical Suggestions

1. President Andrew Jackson: Jackson might be impeached on grounds that he violated the Constitution by taking over powers granted to the other two branches of the federal government. Jackson destroyed the Second Bank of the U.S., which had been created by laws passed by Congress. He also ignored the Supreme Court's decision concerning the Cherokee Indians when he used military troops to force the Indians out of Georgia on the Trail of Tears to the Indian Territory (later Oklahoma).

2. President Andrew Johnson: The House of Representatives impeached Johnson on February 24, 1868. The main charge against him was that he had violated the Tenure of Office Act by firing Secretary of War Edwin Stanton without the consent of the Senate. Aspects of his violation of that Act were the subject of 10 of the 11 impeachment charges against Johnson. The motive behind Johnson's impeachment was to punish him for opposing the harsh plan for Reconstruction that the Radical Republicans in Congress wanted to impose on the South after the Civil War. Johnson favored a version of the more lenient plan that Lincoln had proposed before his assassination. Had Johnson been convicted, the Senate's President Pro Tempore, Benjamin Wade, would have succeeded him as President, and the Radical Republicans would have controlled both the executive and legislative branches of the federal government.

   Article I: "That said Andrew Johnson, President of the United States, on the 21st day of February ... 1868 ... unmindful of the high duties of his office, of his oath of office, and of the requirement of the Constitution that he should take care that the laws be faithfully executed, did unlawfully and in violation of the Constitution and laws of the United States ... order in writing for the removal of Edwin M. Stanton from the office of Secretary for the Department of War ...."

   Article II: "That said Andrew Johnson ... did attempt to bring into disgrace, ridicule, hatred, contempt, and reproach the Congress of the United States and ... make and deliver with a loud voice certain intemperate, inflammatory and scandalous harangues ... amid the cries, jeers and laughter of the multitudes then assembled."

3. President Ulysses S. Grant: charges against Grant could be based on the corruption and scandals during his administration. Grant's private secretary was involved in the 1875 Whiskey Ring scandal that prevented the Treasury from collecting millions of dollars of tax revenue. Dozens of Grant's in-laws became public employees at a time when the Civil Service Commission was very weak. Secretary of War Belknap sold the right to distribute goods to the Indians to greedy merchants, gaining $24,000 in the process. Grant agreed not to release Treasury gold into circulation when Jim Fisk and Jay Gould tried to corner the market on gold.

4. President Warren G. Harding: Secretary of the Interior Albert B. Fall allegedly leased government oil reserves at Teapot Dome, Wyoming, to private businessmen Harry F. Sinclair and Edward L. Doheney in return for a "loan" of $400,000 from the two men. Charles R. Forbes, a Harding appointee, stole $200 million from the Veterans Bureau, largely through contracts for building hospitals. The Senate investigated Attorney General Daughtery for the illegal sale of pardons and liquor permits. Two other persons committed suicide as a result of the discovery of other scandals.

Name _____

Mock Impeachment Trials–
Historical Suggestions

5. President Franklin D. Roosevelt: After the Japanese bombed Pearl Harbor, Roosevelt issued an executive order that forced the evacuation of Japanese Americans from their homes on the West Coast into internment camps in the interior of the U.S. Over one hundred thousand people, at least two-thirds of whom were native-born American citizens, were forced to sell their homes and businesses at prices below market value and were imprisoned without trial. Although the Supreme Court upheld Roosevelt's actions in this 1944 case of Korematsu vs. United States, Congress apologized to the Japanese Americans and provided reparations money several decades later. A mock impeachment trial of Roosevelt might be based on his violating the Constitution's Bill of Rights by depriving Japanese Americans of liberty and property without due process of law.

6. President Lyndon B. Johnson: Johnson might be impeached over the Gulf of Tonkin incident. Evidence now exists that shows that the incident Johnson used to get the Gulf of Tonkin Resolution passed by Congress and to more deeply involve the U.S. in the Vietnam conflict was not an attack on U.S. ships and that Johnson knew it wasn't when he made his national address in August 1964. Johnson might be impeached on a charge of providing misleading information to the public and to Congress in order to wrest war powers from Congress that were not given to the President by the Constitution.

7. President Richard M. Nixon: The Watergate scandal began in June 1972 with a break-in at the Democratic party's headquarters by persons working for the Committee to Reelect the President (Nixon). The purpose of the break-in was to steal campaign plans from the Democrats in order to increase Nixon's chances of being reelected. Nixon would have been impeached because of bribery and obstruction of justice when it was finally proven that, within a week of the break-in, he was paying the burglars money to keep quiet about the crime and about who had ordered it. During the two-year course of the scandal, the press and the Senate Investigating Committee uncovered many other illegal or unethical practices of Nixon's administration. Nixon resigned effective August 9, 1974, before the House impeached him. The following are the articles on which he would have been impeached:

Article I: "In his conduct of the office of President of the United States, Richard M. Nixon, in violation of his constitutional oath faithfully to execute the office of President of the United States and, to the best of his ability, preserve, protect, and defend the Constitution of the United States, and in violation of his constitutional duty to take care that the laws be faithfully executed, has prevented, obstructed, and impeded the administration of justice ...."

Article II: "Using the powers of the office of President of the United States, Richard M. Nixon, in violation of his constitutional oath ... and in disregard of his constitutional duty to take care that the laws be faithfully executed, has repeatedly engaged in conduct violating the constitutional rights of citizens, impairing the due and proper administration of justice and the conduct of lawful inquiries, or contravening the laws governing agencies of the executive branch and purposes of these agencies."

26

Mock Impeachment Trials– Historical Suggestions

Article III: "In his conduct of the office of President of the United States, Richard M. Nixon, contrary to his oath faithfully to execute the office of President of the United States . . . has failed without lawful cause or excuse to produce papers and things as directed by duly authorized subpoenas issued by the Committee on the Judiciary of the House of Representatives . . . . In refusing to produce these papers and things Richard M. Nixon . . . interposed the powers of the presidency against the lawful subpoenas of the House of Representatives, thereby assuming to himself functions and judgments necessary to the exercise of the sole power of impeachment vested by the Constitution in the House of Representatives."

8. President Ronald Reagan: Reagan may have participated in or known about a scheme, known as the Iran-Contra Affair, in which weapons were sold to Iran (a recent enemy of the U.S.) in order to secretly and illegally finance the anti-government rebels in Nicaragua.

9. President William Jefferson Clinton: Clinton was accused of having had an affair with a young woman who worked as an intern at the White House. When information about the affair became public, various people and official groups questioned Clinton about the situation. Some people thought Clinton had lied while being questioned, and others thought he had been active in hiding gifts exchanged during the affair. While many people thought Clinton's behavior was immoral and unethical, he wasn't impeached for having had an affair but for lying about the situation and obstructing justice. Clinton was acquitted of both charges of impeachment by a roll call vote of the senators on February 12, 1999.

Article I: "In his conduct while President of the United States, William Jefferson Clinton, in violation of his constitutional oath faithfully to execute the office of President of the United States and, to the best of his ability, preserve, protect, and defend the Constitution of the United States, and in violation of his constitutional duty to take care that the laws be faithfully executed, has willfully corrupted and manipulated the judicial process of the United States for his personal gain and exoneration impeding the administration of justice, in that . . . (he) . . . provided perjurious false and misleading testimony to the grand jury. . . ."

Article II: "In his conduct while President of the United States, William Jefferson Clinton, in violation of his constitutional oath . . . and in violation of his constitutional duty to take care that the laws be faithfully executed, has prevented, obstructed, and impeded the administration of justice, and has to that end engaged personally, and through his subordinates and agents, in a course of conduct or scheme designed to delay, impede, cover up, and conceal the existence of evidence and testimony related to a Federal civil rights action brought against him in a duly instituted judicial proceeding."

Internet Research Ideas

1. Matthew Brady is well known for his photographs of Abraham Lincoln and the Civil War. Find some of Brady's pictures on the internet and make an album with captions for the photographs and historical information to accompany them.

2. Research one or more of the presidential election campaigns. Write a report, make a scrapbook or do a comparison/contrast paper on the issues, slogans, advertising techniques, political parties, campaign strategies and distribution of votes.

3. Several Presidents were generals before they became President. Research the military careers of (a) George Washington, (b) Andrew Jackson, (c) William Henry Harrison, (d) Zachary Taylor, (e) Ulysses S. Grant, (f) Dwight D. Eisenhower or (g) Theodore Roosevelt with the Rough Riders during the Spanish-American War.

4. President Theodore Roosevelt is well known for his conservation efforts in the West. Find out about his work with Gifford Pinchot and the conservationist John Muir.

5. President Andrew Jackson had been an Indian fighter and disliked Indians. Jackson overrode the Supreme Court decision about Cherokee lands in Georgia and forced the Indians to march on the Trail of Tears from Georgia to Oklahoma.

6. Presidential assassinations might interest some students. Research (a) Abraham Lincoln, (b) James A. Garfield, (c) William McKinley or (d) John F. Kennedy.

7. Several Presidents also survived assassination attempts. (a) Ronald Reagan was seriously wounded by John W. Hinkley on March 30, 1981. (b) Theodore Roosevelt was shot on October 14, 1912. He was saved from death by objects in his coat pocket. (c) An assassination attempt on Franklin D. Roosevelt on February 15, 1933, resulted in the death of Chicago mayor Anton J. Cermak. (d) Two assassination attempts were directed at Gerald Ford. On September 5, 1975, Lynette Alice ("Squeaky") Fromm tried to kill Ford. Sara Jane Moore made the second attempt on Ford's life on September 22, 1975, in San Francisco, California. (e) Harry S. Truman escaped death at the hands of two Puerto Rican nationalists on November 1, 1950.

8. Many well-known and worthy men ran for President but were never elected. Research the political career and presidential races of one of the following: (a) Henry Clay, the Great Compromiser, ran for President three times in 1824, 1832 and 1844. He is known for the Missouri Compromise, the Compromise Tariff of 1833 and the Compromise of 1850, which postponed the Civil War. (b) William Jennings Bryan, leader of the Populist Party and Secretary of State under Wilson, also ran three times, in 1860, 1900 and 1908. (c) Thomas E. Dewey ran against Franklin D. Roosevelt in 1944 and against Harry S. Truman in 1948. (d) Adlai Stevenson competed against Dwight Eisenhower in 1952 and 1956. (e) Horace Greeley, the newspaper editor, ran against Ulysses S. Grant in 1872. (f) The Socialist party leader Eugene V. Debs ran for President in 1904, 1908, 1912 and 1920. He even received votes from faithful party members when he was in prison during the 1920 election. (g) Aaron Burr ran in the elections of 1796 and 1800. He is better known for killing Alexander Hamilton in a duel and for being tried for treason.

9. Three Presidents later had careers in other branches of government. (a) John Quincy Adams served in the House of Representatives. (b) William Howard Taft was Chief Justice of the Supreme Court. (c) Andrew Johnson was a senator from Tennessee.

10. In 1906, Theodore Roosevelt became the first American to win a Nobel Peace prize. Find out how he helped end the Russo-Japanese War in 1905.

11. Some Presidents have been so strong that they dominated the other two branches of the national government. Choose one of the following to research and show how he gained power, what he did with it and how he affected the other two branches: (a) Andrew Jackson, (b) Abraham Lincoln, (c) Theodore Roosevelt, (d) Franklin D. Roosevelt, (e) Lyndon B. Johnson and (f) Richard M. Nixon.

12. Research the White House to find out its history, what offices are in the East and West Wings, when the tours are, how the public rooms are decorated, what state functions are held there and where the First Family's rooms are.

13. Research one of the Cabinet departments to find out its history, some of its famous secretaries, the agencies under its control and its budget. E-mail the secretary of that department about issues that interest you.

14. Although no woman has yet been elected President, several have campaigned for the office. Research (a) Shirley Chisholm in the 1972 or (b) Elizabeth Dole in 1999.

15. Many First Ladies have greatly influenced their husbands and the nation. Some women to research are (a) Abigail Adams, (b) Dolley Madison, (c) Eleanor Roosevelt, (d) Rosalynn Carter, (e) Jacqueline Kennedy, (f) Nancy Reagan or (g) Hillary Rodham Clinton.

16. The National Weather Service and the National Oceanic and Atmospheric Administration provide information about the weather. Look up their web sites to find what maps, forecasts, statistics and live camera views they provide.

17. During Andrew Johnson's impeachment trial in 1868, seven Radical Republicans broke from their party and voted to acquit Johnson. Read about Edmond Ross, the Republican who cast the deciding vote in the trial in President Kennedy's *Profiles in Courage*. Find out his political fate and those of the other seven men.

Multiple Intelligence Activities

Linguistic Intelligence

1. Memorize and give a dramatic interpretation of a famous presidential speech such as Lincoln's Second Inaugural Address, John F. Kennedy's Inaugural Address, Woodrow Wilson's speech about the Fourteen Points or Franklin D. Roosevelt's message to Congress asking for a declaration of war against Japan.

2. Assume the role of presidential press secretary and write a statement to the media to comment on a historical or current issue in government. You could also be the President's speech writer and write this year's State of the Union Address for the President to deliver on television.

Visual/Spatial Intelligence

1. Use portraits or photographs of Presidents as models to sketch your own drawings of these men. Take this a step further by drawing caricatures of the Presidents or political cartoons about events that occurred during their administrations.

2. Design new uniforms for the military band that plays "Hail to the Chief" when the President appears on formal occasions.

3. Design a monument to honor one of the Presidents. Some examples you might want to look at before doing your own drawing are the Lincoln Memorial, the Jefferson Memorial, the Washington Monument, the proposed Franklin D. Roosevelt Memorial and Mount Rushmore.

Auditory Intelligence

1. (a) Learn the presidential theme song "Hail to the Chief," and play it on a musical instrument for the class. (b) Rewrite "Hail to the Chief" in a different musical style: rock, jazz, classical or country, for example. (c) Write a completely new theme song for the President with lyrics. Choose your own style.

2. As President, you can invite almost any musician to the White House to perform for a public occasion. Pretend that you are welcoming a head of state to the White House for a state dinner and a public performance. Plan the show for the President: what musicians will appear, what music will they play, what is the order in which the pieces are presented, what music will pay tribute to the country of the head of state?

Mathematical Intelligence

1. Several presidential elections were very close in their popular votes. Two examples are (a) the Kennedy-Nixon election in 1960 and (b) the Nixon-Humphrey election in 1968. Research these or other close elections and find out where the change in the popular vote might have changed the election results. Demonstrate your findings on a chart, map or graph showing the distribution of votes.

2. The vote by the Electoral College occurs after the popular election and is what determines who will actually become President. Although it has become customary for the electors to vote for the same candidate who won the popular vote in their state, the concept of winner-

Multiple Intelligence Activities

takes-all distorts the results of the people's votes. Pick two or three elections and show through charts, graphs, maps or other mathematical models the difference winner-takes-all makes between the popular vote and the Electoral College's vote.

3. After doing research on the current U.S. budget, draw up a simplified budget of your own. Be sure to include such categories as defense spending, Social Security and Medicare payments, welfare, education, roads and paying interest on the national debt. Illustrate your proposed budget with charts or graphs.

Kinesthetic Intelligence

1. Learn one or more dances popular during various Presidents' terms and perform them for your class or teach them to classmates. Some choices of dances include the Charleston, Twist, waltz, minuet, country reels, swing, jitterbug, the Lindy and disco.

2. Find out about some of the tactics the Secret Service officers use to protect the President's life and about their training. Explain or demonstrate to your classmates what you learned.

Interpersonal Intelligence

1. Hold a press conference in which one person is the President, another the press secretary and the rest of the class are reporters. Students should research and write out questions about national events and issues before the press conference is held. The press secretary can write and deliver an opening statement on a "hot" current topic. The President would then answer questions from the reporters.

2. Hold a mock Cabinet meeting. Pick a current situation or a historical event like planning for World War II or making a decision about the Cuban Missile Crisis. Each secretary tells what his or her department can do to resolve the crisis.

Intrapersonal Intelligence

1. Write a series of letters from a President to his friends or several diary entries from a President describing his feelings and doubts as he struggles with difficult events and decisions. Here are some suggested topics: (a) George Washington's precedent-setting decisions as first President of the U.S., (b) Woodrow Wilson's struggle with the Senate over ratifying the Treaty of Versailles and joining the League of Nations, (c) Nixon's efforts to remain in office as more and more information about Watergate became public, (d) Andrew Jackson's grief at the death of his wife before his first inauguration, (e) Thomas Jefferson's decisions (such as buying the Louisiana Territory and fighting the Barbary Pirates) that went against his deepest political beliefs, (f) Abraham Lincoln's efforts to control his Cabinet and to find good generals during the Civil War and (g) Lyndon B. Johnson's work to create laws to safeguard civil rights for African Americans.

Answer Key

Executive Department Questions, page 9

1. A candidate for the presidency or vice presidency must be at least 35 years old, a native-born citizen of the U.S. and have been a resident of the U.S. for at least 14 years.

2. The number of the electors is equal to the number of representatives plus the number of senators a state has in Congress. Answers to the second question will vary by state.

3. One presidential term is four years. A President can be elected to only two terms. The Vice President can serve two terms in his own right.

4. The Constitution made the rule about salary changes to keep the Legislative Branch from controlling the Executive Branch. Congress cannot bribe a President into doing its bidding or punish him for disagreeing with it.

5. The President can make treaties or make appointments of Supreme Court justices, Cabinet members and ambassadors only with the advice and consent of the Senate.

6. The President's duties are to periodically inform Congress about the state of the Union, to receive ambassadors and ministers from other countries, to make sure the laws are faithfully executed and to commission all military officers.

7. The Constitution does not describe the powers or duties of the Vice President.

8. a. If the President commits crimes, Congress can remove him by the impeachment process. b. If the President is disabled, he can write a letter to the President Pro Tempore of the Senate and the Speaker of the House saying he is disabled. He will then be relieved of his duties. If the President is unable or unwilling to send the letter, the Vice President and the majority of the Cabinet send a letter to the required officials; then the Vice President takes over the job.

Presidential and Constitutional Trivia, page 10

1. President Nixon resigned before he was impeached, so the rule about not being able to pardon an impeachment did not apply to President Ford.

2. Truman could have run for President a second time. Amendment 22 said that its provisions did not apply to the President who was in office at the time that amendment was ratified. (Congress did not intend to use the amendment as leverage to control Truman's administration.)

3. Since the South claimed to have left the Union, the only power Lincoln could have over the Confederacy was by force of arms in his role as commander in chief of the military.

4. Burr was not convicted because the Constitution requires that there be two witnesses to the same act of treason, and there was only one witness against him.

5. Having been born in Czechoslovakia, Mrs. Albright is not a native-born citizen of the U.S., so she can never become President.

6. The election went to the House of Representatives to be decided.

7. No. There is nothing in the Constitution that prevents a woman from becoming President.

8. Wilson would not have completed his second term. His Vice President and the majority of his Cabinet would have declared him incapable of carrying out his duties.

Presidential Powers and Duties, pages 11-12

1. Yes. He is commander in chief of the militias of the states when they are called into national service.

2. Yes. He can do both things. He shall deliver to Congress information about the state of the Union. He may require the opinion of the heads of his Cabinet departments.

3. No. None. (Justices are removed only by death, resignation or conviction on impeachment charges.)

4. No. None. (He cannot use his office to harass private citizens.)

5. Yes. He can make treaties with foreign countries with the consent of the Senate.

6. Yes. He shall make sure that the laws of the nation are faithfully executed.

7. No. None. (The President does not have the power to pardon impeachment cases.)

8. Yes. He is commander in chief of the U.S. army and navy.

9. Yes. He can appoint persons to positions in the Executive Branch while the Senate is in recess.

Presidential Roles, page 14

1. B, 2. C, 3. A, 4. B, 5. D, 6. F, 7. E, 8. C, 9. B, 10. E, 11. C, 12. G, 13. B

Separation of Powers, pages 15-16

1. yes, 2. no, 3. yes, 4. no, 5. yes, 6. yes, 7. yes, 8. yes, 9. no

Checks and Balances Questions, page 18

1. yes, 2. yes, 3. yes, 4. yes, 5. no

Presidential Cabinet Questions, page 21

1. Department of Energy
2. Department of Housing and Urban Development
3. Department of Veterans Affairs
4. Department of Health and Human Services
5. Department of State
6. Department of Transportation
7. Department of Labor
8. Department of Treasury

Presidential Ranking, page 22

Answers to all of these questions will vary depending on the students' knowledge, research and opinions about the Presidents.

TLC10243 Copyright © Teaching & Learning Company, Carthage, IL 62321-0C